Do We Resemble Our Father

RODNEY K. ADAMS

Do We Resemble Our Father
Rodney K. Adams

Cover Design By: Jazzy Kitty Publishing
Cover Photograph by: Jazzy Kitty Publishing
Logo Designs By: Andre M. Saunders
Editor: Anelda L. Attaway

© 2011 Rodney K. Adams 1-744240113
ISBN 978-0-9843255-9-7
Library of Congress Control Number: 2012936428

All rights reserved. This book is protected under the copyright laws of the United States of America. This book may not be copied or reprinted for commercial gain or profit. The use of short quotations or occasional page copying for personal or group study is permitted and encouraged. Permission will be granted upon request. Bible scriptural references are taken from the King James Version, New Living Translation, and the Life Application Study Bible.

For Worldwide Distribution. Printed in the United States of America. Published by Jazzy Kitty Greetings Marketing & Publishing, LLC. Utilizing Microsoft Publishing Software.

ACKNOWLEGMENTS

To God, our Father, be all glory, honor, thanks, and praise. Great things He has done!

This is the day that the Lord has made! Let us rejoice and be glad in it. I would like to give thanks to my brothers and sisters in the ministry who continually aid me in this gospel journey.

Thank you Brittany, when I started this, you volunteered to write as the Lord guided me to speak.

Jermaine Lewis for helping in sponsoring this book.

My mother Lucille for her help with the editing and "bringing it home".

Thank you family, friends and many organizations for the cards, letters, and care packages while serving in the military.

Finally, to my family and friends who have stood by my side when the "chips were down". I love you all with the love of God!

DEDICATIONS

This book is dedicated to God's children who walk on water.

TABLE OF CONTENTS

INTRODUCTION..i
CHAPTER 1 Our Ordered Purpose..................................01
CHAPTER 2 Guilty By Association...............................12
CHAPTER 3 According To... Who Told You?...............24
CHAPTER 4 Fear versus Focus......................................34
CHAPTER 5 Father's Day...43
ABOUT THE AUTHOR..52

INTRODUCTION

How does the world view you? If that seems far-fetched, how does your community feel about you? Neighbors? What about friends or family? Whether you are walking in the park, driving to a video store, attending church services, music concerts, restaurants, any place in time, is there something different about your character? As we live our everyday lives, do we see our Father in Heaven living through each of us?

It is important to God how the world views Christians because it reflects a direct relationship to the Father. God draws all to Him through His Son. (John 12:32) However, the decision is left up to us to accept a personal relationship with God through His Son, Jesus Christ. Jesus referred to this foundation of portraying God to the world in the gospel of John 12:14. *"He that believes on me, believes not on me, but on Him that sent me and he that sees me sees Him that sent me."* It is important that God be glorified in all of creation so that God is seen as the all in all, Alpha and Omega, the beginning and the end. Jesus instructed that in order for the world to see the Father in us, we must start by believing and accepting what He (Jesus) taught. The only way to the Father is through our Lord and Savior Jesus Christ. In John 14:6 Jesus says, *"I am the way, truth, and the life. No man comes unto the Father but by me."* God wants a personal relationship with each of us through Jesus. While different ethnic groups practice varied spiritual theologies, the apostle Paul says in 1 Corinthians chapter 10, to imitate his way of growing closer to a Christ-centered life. It is important to follow closely to those who have a clear perception of God's plan. As we grow in Christ, God is able to reveal Himself through us. How can we tell who has a clear perception of God's will? We will know by the fruit, which is attitude and character they portray, manifestations, or living proof, of God's Holy Spirit. (Galatians 5:22) Therefore, we must continuously seek and demonstrate the Word of God which leads us to unto all Truth. Ultimately Jesus is **the *only* true path to God**-to that end, the relationship between the Father and the Son is perfect. While we are not perfect in our lives because of sin, we understand what God wants through His Holy Spirit AND we have His Word to be a lamp unto our walk as we seek to glorify His presence in our lives. Thanks be to God for His Word! Of course the goal is to accept, grow, and develop this relationship with God. It is not a focus on any specific religion, but a desired relationship that the Father wants with His children, *individually*. The world is full of religion and traditions that guide us into a spiritual existence, but what about displaying God's attributes? When or how does this persona of God shine through our character? Is having an outlook of positive ideas enough? What about our identity or acceptance? Will this work with our life and/or future plans? This may be big shoes to fill, especially since many of us are not looking for 'center stage'. We all have moment by moment situations we encounter, that will test our faith in God. Whether simple or difficult, it is our **response** to that situation that defines our character.

Summarily, this was written to inspire hope, strengthen faith, to provide guidance into God as our Father. Rest assured that God wants to be seen of His grace and mercy from *all* levels and walks of life, in Heaven and Earth. Whether you are a motivational speaker that can recite a thousand words, that person with a million dollar smile, or if you feel you have nothing to smile about, God wants to display Himself through you.

Do We Resemble Our Father

Chapter 1

Our Ordered Purpose

God's plan is for us to find our purpose in His will, to display His grace and true nature through Jesus Christ. (2 Timothy 1:9) In so doing, will discover our specific goals as we develop a closer relationship with Him as it is mentioned in Romans 12:2. Matthew 28:18, Jesus speaks to His disciples saying, *"All power is given unto me in heaven and earth. Go ye therefore and teach all nations, baptizing them in the name of the Father, and of the Son, and of the Holy Spirit, teaching them to observe all things whatsoever I have commanded you. And, lo, I am with you always, even unto the end of the world amen."* It is important that we follow this commission with Jesus as our guide, so that our lives will be a direct reflection of God living through us. *"He that has my commandments and keeps them, it is he that loves me. And he that loves me shall be loved of my Father, and I will love him and will manifest myself in him."* John 14:21. More and more as we read through scripture, Jesus speaks of showing Himself to the world

Do We Resemble Our Father

through us!

From the moment of birth, as infants, we absorb knowledge about our environment. In fact, beginning stage of life is a teachable state. We learn from speaking our native tongue, to walking, riding a bike and so on. As we grow from infant to adult, information is gained through our senses; reasoning and natural revelation are experienced through society. There are different stages in our lives, in different areas, where we feel we have reached utopia and conclude that no more can be learned, or to continue pursuing a certain topic may be a waste of time. Where we were once teachable, or in a learning phase, we become over confident, possibly arrogant in what is believed as truth. We must be careful not to become complacent and not teachable as we grow. Whether we are beginning Christians or 'seasoned veterans', we must allow Jesus Christ to show us the way. There is *always* room to grow and expand in spiritual knowledge, remembering that like Christ, we become teachers of His Word.

Teaching shows a passion and concern for passing on what is learned. The primary goal for those who teach in any area of studies is that their students gain an

Do We Resemble Our Father

understanding to the subject being taught. Conclusively a deep satisfaction comes when a student correctly displays what the teacher has taught. Our Father in Heaven *wants* us to know about Him. But, we must be teachable and willing to learn the plan laid out for us.

In John 3:1, Nicodemus learned this lesson well! We are introduced to him as a Pharisee and member of the ruling high council. Pharisees were a group of religious leaders whom Jesus and John the Baptist often criticized for their viewpoints on religion. Many Pharisees were jealous of Jesus because He challenged their authority. Nicodemus was an educated teacher well known for his knowledge of scripture. But even Nicodemus felt that there was still truth to be learned and he believed that Jesus had the answers! So he went to learn about Christ. Nicodemus could have sent one of his assistants but he wanted to know the facts for himself.

What was his purpose for seeking Christ? Like many searching for truth, initially we find ourselves uncomfortable. Nicodemus positioned himself to learn about Jesus by visiting Him at night, possibly not to be seen. Whether we come to Christ boldly or in the still of the

Do We Resemble Our Father

moment, Jesus is always available for us, anytime or anywhere. As he learned about the gospel of Christ, Nicodemus' life began to change. At first, he taught openly the Law of Moses, but remained in the background when it came to speaking of the gospel of Christ. However in John 7:51, Nicodemus took a stand for Christ in the presence of the council saying he (Jesus) deserves a fair trial before passing judgment. This may seem a small task for some, but for Nicodemus this was a major accomplishment. In the same manner as Nicodemus, no matter the inconveniences we face on our journey, we must hurdle the obstacles to seek, learn, and apply the plan of salvation. Everyone has a purpose and each is important to God no matter the size of the task. Just as Christ assured the disciples that He would *always* be with them, the same blessed assurance of salvation given to Nicodemus, is also given to us.

Sometimes it is not easy to follow orders or stick to plans. Especially since our journey consists of a conversion from the physical life to the eternal life - *prescribed by God (the bible), ordained by Christ (by authority), and manifested in the Holy Spirit (living witness)*. We prefer to design our own 'hassle free' journey. Why not consider an

Do We Resemble Our Father

alternate solution as long as it 'fixes' the situation? In this technological age, we look for quick solutions to solve problems. Unfortunately, the upshot of a 'quick fix' is that it can mask the underlying problem that needs complete restoration. Sure, it may look good on paper, but in the long run may have damaging effects. Such is the situation with the prodigal son because he decided to try things his way.

In Luke 15:11, the Prodigal Son's journey begins with Jesus explaining about a man with two sons. The younger son decided he wanted his share of his father's inheritance. Even though he knew his father was just, fair and displayed positive values, he was not willing to wait until the father was ready to pass on the estate to his children. The younger son also learned over the years that his father was not poor. He owned property, livestock, even the servants had extra to give to unfortunate people. Maybe he felt that he could manage his portion and enjoy life. Who needs rules? Why is having order and structure important? It is clear that the younger son wanted immediate satisfaction of enjoying the fruits of his labor. He was not getting any younger and could plainly see his older brother following the path of his father, so why not try something different. Could his father

Do We Resemble Our Father

be too controlling or over protective? Whatever his reasoning, the younger son was ready to start his life separate from his father.

Now parents naturally want to shield their children from harm. We are not given a historical viewpoint of the father's life growing up, but are made known of his financial status. Also, there is no account of the father's personal experiences dealing with this type of situation. All we see is a father that realizes his son is willfully set to leave on his own. The father of the younger son gives him his portion and lets him go. Understand that God will not force Himself upon us. In the first chapter of Romans, it mentions that if we choose a destructive path, God will not stand in the way. But there are consequences, for the penalty for sin is death. (Romans 6:23)

Later, the son came to his senses and realized the huge mistake he made. He comes back asking forgiveness for what he has done. The father is overjoyed and celebrates his return. God is *always* ready for us to come to Him. If we get lost along the way, He is *always* ready for us to return to Him. Also note what is important for those who remain with God. The older son in the story was jealous of

Do We Resemble Our Father

his brother's celebration, but his father reminded him of his relationship that he has with the older son. He also added that the older son is the rightful heir of *all* the father owns. The spiritual analysis of this story, does indeed remind us that as Christians, our Father in Heaven, our Creator, owns everything and has called us heirs to His kingdom. All that God has and all that He is, He freely gives to those who remain in Him. However, we must not envy others, or respond in a negative manner when someone is blessed with a home, car or a promotion. Especially when we do not perceive any indication of our "Prayers being answered." It could be a test to see your response to their situation. Yes, we have different circumstances good and bad. One thing is for sure, be glad for those who make it through tough times, because God has not forgotten you.

Rejoice when the lost have found their way. (Luke 15:7) When we fall short of our goals, it is not comfortable to be seen as a disappointment. We must uplift others as we are being uplifted as well. We give thanks to God, and make use of what we have received for the will of God. Someone who has been promoted to a stronger position may be able to help other co-workers, the community, or

Do We Resemble Our Father

the business itself. It may not be for us to see or know the end result of our actions, but we should remain encouraged to plant seeds of faithfulness or initiate innovative ideas that inspire others.

I remember watching the movie, *The Prince of Egypt,* in which Zipporah's father sang about how each person is like a strand of cloth. As our lives are woven, we may not see the end result of a beautiful tapestry, but we will understand our part or purpose in life and God's vision.

Just as teachers experience a high degree of satisfaction when their students excel, we also feel a sense of accomplishment when we complete a task or goal. Even though our tasks are often difficult and we experience a feeling of wanting to give up, we are encouraged with words of our blessed Savior. In Matthew 11:28 Jesus says, *"Come to me all who labor and are heavy laden, I will give you rest."* While the answers to our trials may not come quickly, we are encouraged that Christ is the answer! When our minds fill with worry or our hearts experience brokenness, we can hold on to the assurance that Christ is peace and the ultimate healer. We get angry sometimes bitter. Our Savior is joy and the compassion. Sometimes we

Do We Resemble Our Father

give up, but Jesus endures forever. He took on the sins of the world from beginning to end, that we may be saved. Jesus experienced the hurt, sadness, depression, disappointments, pain and separation, that we would not be alone. For the prodigal son, he realized his true resources were with his family, so he returned to the home of his father and remained with him.

What is the purpose for us as we spread the gospel of Christ? If we are to learn about God we must seek after Him and not rely on someone else to do it for us. Each one of us are unique-our DNA separates us individually. No two fingerprints are alike. Amazing! There is a plan and purpose for each of us. It only makes sense that we receive our instructions as they pertain to our lives personally from God. When we allow Jesus to lead us with instruction and direction, it will bring us together unified in faith under the direction of God's Holy Spirit. Jesus prayed for all generations to come in John 17:20-21 saying, *"I am praying not only for these disciples but also for all who will ever believe in me through their message. I pray that they will all be one, just as you and I are one, as you are in me, Father, and I am in you. And they may be in us so that the*

Do We Resemble Our Father

world will believe You sent me."

As we strengthen and develop our relationship with God, our purpose will be revealed as He reveals Himself to us. It is important for children of God to know their Father! The spiritual family is important with its prayer structure from God to endure the weaknesses of sin. (Matthew 6:9-13) Equally important, we must respect and uphold the earthly family that God placed us while we journey here on Earth. With our earthly family, we understand ourselves better when we have the opportunity to know our heritage. Without understanding family structure whether physical or spiritual, there are missing pieces to the puzzle of life. Establishing a relationship with Jesus, helps to "fill in the gaps" in our thought patterns and actions that are contrary to living *healthy* in the Lord. Sure we become productive citizens. Whether material riches are acquired or not, what is being destroyed is the importance and knowledge of our "Heavenly heritage."

In Genesis 25:33, Esau traded his birthright, or inheritance, to his younger brother for a bowl of stew. Apparently for Esau, his "birth order" as the oldest son meant nothing to him. Esau's decision to satisfy his

Do We Resemble Our Father

physical needs destroyed his father's (Isaac) lifetime plans for him. Esau did not consider the importance of long-honored tradition of family inheritance. His father's blessings were less important than satisfying his immediate need! Do we, likewise, miss God's blessings when we submit to greed, selfishness, or self indulgence to satisfy our immediate need?

Human satisfaction is based on our five senses. Generally, we seek instant gratification based on what we see, hear, taste, touch or smell.

Now different from Esau, Jacob, the younger brother, valued and "embraced" the concept of the *firstborn rights*. Such is our relationship with God. It is important to see that God is not only concerned about who is born first, but who will accept a right relationship with Him! Who will inherit the kingdom of God? Those who will not deny being a child of God. As you seek your purpose, begin by accepting who you are and to whom you belong. Romans 12:2 says, *do not copy the behavior and ways of the world, but let God into your heart and guide your steps. In so doing, you will learn and know God's will for you which is good, pleasing and perfect to God.*

Chapter 2

Guilty By Association

"Even before He made the world, God loved us and chose us in Christ to be holy and without fault in His eyes. God decided in advance to adopt us into His own family by bringing us to Himself through Jesus Christ. This is what He wanted to do, and it gave Him great pleasure." (Ephesians 1:4-5)

Who do we belong to? Even before the world was formed, God knew Satan would launch an attack on Him and His creation, but God had a plan. So why is family important to God and what does it mean to be a part of His family? I remember talking with a relative about family associations. As children growing up in our community, our relationship to the family was known by reference of the parents' or grandparents' names to our names. My brother, sister and I were introduced as Ellen's grandchildren in her town. At home it was Billy's kids for our dad or Sweetie's kids for mom. We were also known as Barber kinfolk when discussing family origins or reunions.

Do We Resemble Our Father

I did not understand why my first name was not used a lot, until it was time for chores. Even so, that did not bother me too much. However, I thought these neighbors must know my parents, *and* my birthday is coming up, *and* I really want that green machine, *so* I better behave! For those who may not know, the green machine was the next generation big wheel.

Moving on, two "ideologies" have caused the sinful destruction of families:

First, the anxiety to leave home because we feel there is something missing from our view of a perfect home. Our thoughts focus on a comparison of how our parents did things and what we would do differently, or possibly better. We continuously view our current parental environment as to how "We are going to act as parents." Yes, children do watch and listen! Parental or adult skills may move to the opposite end of the spectrum, over indulging, thereby responding to *all* of their children's requests. This is one of the parent-child themes that surfaces in the story of the prodigal son and likewise, a very important concept is missed: ***having a little guidance, as opposed to none, do assist in problem solving.***

Do We Resemble Our Father

Secondly, and in a more direct manner, abuse takes on many forms whether physically or mentally. Sadly, some abuse may be accepted as a way of life with no hope of escape, living day by day in a 'hell house'. The results can be abysmal as well. Abused children often become abusive parents. Violent behavior becomes second-natured. Children from all ages may be left to care for themselves.

Because we sin against God, our spiritual association with Him is cut off. In order to bring salvation to mankind, or repair our broken relationship with God, our Father had to come to where we are, through the birth of His Son Jesus, in order to reunite us with God's Holy Spirit. Hebrews 2:14-18 says, *"Because God's children are human beings, made of flesh and blood, the Son also became flesh and blood. For only as a human being could he die, and only by dying could He destroy the power of the devil, who had the power of death. Only in this way could He set free all who have lived their lives as slaves in sin to the fear of dying. We also know that the Son did not come to help angels; He came to help the descendants of Abraham. Therefore, it was necessary for Him to be made in every respect like us, His brothers and sisters, so that He could be our merciful and faithful High Priest before God. Then He could offer a sacrifice that would take away the sins of the people. Since He himself has gone through suffering and testing, He is able to help us when we are tested."*

Time after time. Generation after generation. From the Garden of Eden in the book of Genesis, until the time of Jesus' return in the book of Revelation, Satan wants us to focus on conflictive personality traits such as being ego-centered, self righteous, inconsiderate, one-sided, destructive, and judgmental. These traits not only weakens faith and hope within ourselves, but also breaks down the meaning of God's family with the 'house from hell'. Many have lost hope and looked to other means of peace or happiness. Possibly because their past was full of trauma, the present filled with drama, and nothing to look forward to. First, Satan wants us to believe that a relationship with God is flawed, lacking the resources needed to make it complete, therefore, it is not necessary to be in the family of God. Secondly, we had better be careful because God will confuse and disappoint us, leave us down and out, unloved, unwanted, discouraged and depressed, *and* God

Do We Resemble Our Father

needs us, as His children, to fix it; by *separating ourselves* from Him.

But God intended the family to be a source of acceptance, encouragement, guidance, counsel, healing, respect, communication, and understanding. When we become adults, there is a transition that God wants to take place. These 'family tools' are to be expressed in the world. How can children express what has not been taught them? Our Father wants us to move from the dependent stage to being independent-not as a separate life from Him, but expressing to others about Him. As adults, we are in a continuous state of learning the nature of our Father God. In other words, God continuously teaches so that the world will see the truth about Him-through us! However, when we bring sin and a desire to be independent apart from the essence of God of which we are created, as in Genesis 1:26, we cut ourselves off from God's resources. Just as the prodigal son, we open ourselves to unknown dangers. Satan wants a destruction of the family unit and what it represents. He wants to present God as imperfect and a liar. Since God is for families, Satan wants to wreck havoc on families and show the world that a family is meant to harm

Do We Resemble Our Father

than heal. As we try to build a life to escape hurt, pain or disappointment, we seek other resources to replace the family provisions. We have a natural instinct for a sense of belonging. If it doesn't work at home, we may be close to friends, job associates, peer groups, gangs, or team sports. Anywhere we feel we have peace or happiness. Some may feel a sense of belonging to a church group more than their family. All this is a risk because Satan represents a false sense of security to the truth of reality.

This is how Satan tempted Christ in the wilderness according to Matthew 4:1-11. He wanted Christ to challenge God by taking matters into his own hands, and to seek a relationship outside the family of God. Basically challenge the very essence of who God is. A relationship with the Father is flawed, lacking what Jesus needed to live. Jesus resisted temptation because he knows the Father and he knows himself as His Son and how God operates through him. Jesus essentially told Satan that God cannot be tempted with what is *already* His.

Likewise, it is the same for you and me through God's Holy Spirit and Jesus. We already belong to God! As His children, we have the opportunity to accept what has

Do We Resemble Our Father

already been given. Accepting and living Jesus' lifestyle is the *only* way to resist temptation and resemble the true nature of our Father. Throughout the Gospels in the New Testament of the Bible, Jesus clearly associates his relationship with God the Father. Remember, Satan is out to destroy God's family by any means necessary, using whatever distraction that takes our focus away from God. While drugs or alcohol are obvious distractions, there are others that can hinder our walk in Christ. For clarity, a few mentioned in this text: internet, television, education, church (focusing more on spiritual recognition), jobs or careers, family, friends, money, music, material items as clothing or cars, and not to forget, our own will.

When we place more importance on *anything* more than God, we demonstrate a character weakness, and create a "door" for Satan to **enter** our spirit. Satan uses this methodology and it works for him. Look at how he tempted Adam and Eve.

In Genesis chapter 3, Eve was told by Satan she could make her own decisions, and should take control of her life. Even though God has provided all that Eve needed, she had fallen prey to listening and challenging her Father. Imagine

Do We Resemble Our Father

Satan in a calm dialogue; *"Eve, you are missing something. In fact, God is holding back and being selfish. Eve, you can handle your situations because who knows yourself better than you? You can make your own decisions without any help. You will not lose your life because you will have the knowledge you need to survive! If you are His child, how come you do not have all of what is rightfully yours? Why continue this association with God? What kind of relationship is this where you cannot do this or that? Why wait, Eve take control of your life. Wait for it... wait for it... okay Eve, go now!"*

Talk about peer pressure. Without any self-help literature, history of past mistakes, grading curves, how many of us could have passed that test?

Has anyone felt this way at some point in their life? More so now do I have compassion for our *First Parents* than when I first believed as a Christian. Adam and Eve had God the Father, each other, and what God taught them. We have no excuse for our mistakes because we have been taught from history of ages past. We must seek God first and have faith that He will guide and provide everything we need. (Matthew 6:33)

Do We Resemble Our Father

Remember religion is merely a guide. A **relationship with God** is the goal. Whatever reason we seek after God, the goal is to know God for who He is, and what we are to Him. When the world was created, God *spoke* everything into existence from day and night, Earth and the Sun, to the animals, birds, and the fish in the sea, *everything*! But for Adam, the *only* thing in creation, God looked within Himself and *formed* Adam out of creation! How more perfect can you get than being created *out of* God Himself! God *shaped* Adam and blew the breath of life, *His* breath into Adam! According to Genesis 1:26, **we are all created in God's image and likeness!** *His* character attributes, *His* DNA! The fruits or traits of God that we possess are found in Galatians 5:22-23. There is love, joy, peace, endurance, kindness, goodness, faithfulness, gentleness, and self control. We **are** the result of God expressing Himself in love and creativity in designing a masterpiece. God gave us the best He has, however, we are not satisfied. Because of sin that man has brought into the world, we need the armor of God, as it is listed in Ephesians 6:14-18, to defend God's kingdom or God's *family structure*. These are truth, righteousness, the gospel of peace, faith, salvation, prayer,

Do We Resemble Our Father

and the word of God.

Examining ourselves within humanity, we notice different character attributes that are passed from generation to generation such as genetic traits we possess from our parents, or from family history. But we are also influenced by the neighborhood we live in, our society and nation, and whether we realize this or not, may enhance or deteriorate moral values. According to I Corinthians 12:8-10, there are also spiritual abilities that are given to each of us to carry out God's will. Wisdom to speak truth, knowledge to teach God's word. Faith to endure, the ability to heal, perform miracles, the gift of prophecy. Distinguishing between truth and lies. The ability to speak in tongues or the understanding of it. All of these things have a deciding factor of the type of person we will become; from spiritual traits and abilities, outward influences by society, to genetic traits passed down generations.

Some areas may weigh more on our character traits than others. As our Creator, God knows what is best for each of us and will aide us in becoming the best for Him, for ourselves and others according to His will. If we would

Do We Resemble Our Father

only allow God the opportunity for guidance, our families would be able to survive as God intended. Children would look to parents with assurance rather than impatience. They would look for ways to help their parents, rather than helping themselves depart.

How many of us have "walked" the path of the prodigal son? We may not be satisfied with our conditions, positive home or not. We have ideas that need attention. There are plans that we want to try with our share of funds. Business opportunities, joint ventures, personal entertainment. So many untapped markets. Maybe there is a simple desire of wanting to be loved and or appreciated. But when will the hurting stop? When does the pain or disappointments cease? Where do we go once the home or family is under the destruction of sin? God does not want us to harden our hearts. (Proverbs 28:14) God wants our hearts to be receptive of His Spirit and His law, and to stay out of trouble.

How many relationships have we broken with each other let alone God? Lives that have been severed because we want to go our own way or follow our own ideology. Whether we choose to accept a personal relationship or not,

Do We Resemble Our Father

God is our Creator and has chosen us before the foundation of this world as stated in Ephesians 1:4. It is God's design that we are to live together for eternity, so it is important to God that we know the true meaning of family. As His children in Christ, we *are* to live holy and without fault in His eyes! Our sins are forgiven and God will display Himself through us. How wonderful to be guilty by association! It is not bragging, judging, or criticizing about who is better than the other. It comes down to defending the family of God, our association with Him as His children, Jesus Christ as our Lord and Savior, and each other as brothers and sisters.

Chapter 3

According To... Who Told You?

"That we might walk worthy of the Lord unto all pleasing, being fruitful in every good work and increasing in the knowledge of God. Being strengthened in might <u>according to</u> His glorious power unto all patience and endurance with joyfulness." (Colossians 1:10-11) *"And of His fullness we have all received, and grace for grace."* (John 1:16)

God gives in completion. Nothing else is necessary. God has provided everything we need in existence and Jesus paid the price for sin that separates us from the Father. God is concerned about the status of our relationship with Him. What does it mean that we have all received as a child of God? How does it benefit us? It is unfortunate that many do not care about what God has given us and what He has for us as His children. We go from day to day, living life decided by what we accept as fate or by our own course of action as Eve attempted.

Do We Resemble Our Father

Satan influenced Eve by having her to focus on an ego-centered relationship. The only perspective Satan wanted Eve to see was her own viewpoint of the situation, and the thought of what was lacking from what God had given. Supposedly, Eve's world or environment was not perfect and she should not rely on God who has provided for her. This will lead anyone into a lack of vision which hinders us as well. We fail to see beyond what affects us. We are more concerned with our safety or what we hope to gain because we feel our resources are limited. Next, Satan led Eve to exalt herself, or to make her needs more important than God. Again, we tend to make our problems and situations bigger than what they are. We may place our needs above the will of God. Our neighbor may need a ride to the grocery store, but we are concerned with how much gas is in the tank. A friend or family member may need a little cash to hold over to payday. Do we give out of love, or do we mentally check the balances first before giving? When payday comes, do we mention or hint around for what is due, or simply give praise to God for being able to give?

Adam had a challenging choice to make as well. He decided to accept what Eve had presented. Here we see a

Do We Resemble Our Father

man wanting to be supportive of his wife. She is his soul. Eve had been created out of Adam. Look at the love relationship between these two. Adam surely cherished her above all that had been created. Even though Eve was an extension of Adam's body, mind, heart, and soul, they existed as one according to God's will. Adam loved Eve beyond words could describe and he trusted her with his life. Certainly this woman whom God gave to Adam would not steer him down the wrong path. Adam placed the needs of his spouse before God. Satan tempted Adam with his wife. Now if Adam had been concerned with his surroundings or what he felt was missing in his life, Satan would have tempted him as he did Eve. Men want to have provisions for their family and are concerned with loving their women by pleasing them. Women love their men but are concerned with how the provisions will affect the family. Adam had been given true love but what would happen if he said no to her? Satan knew how to approach both of them. In some life choices we feel our spouse has the best intentions and we want to show support. Remember that God's will comes first and our spouse may be disappointed. We may not be able to see it at first, but in

Do We Resemble Our Father

the long run God's way is the best way.

"By His divine power, God has given us <u>everything</u> we need for living a godly life. We have received all of this by coming to know Him, the One who called us to Himself by means of His marvelous glory and excellence. And because of His glory and excellence, He has given us great and precious promises. These are the promises that <u>enable you to share His divine nature</u> and escape the world's corruption caused by human sin." (2 Peter 1:3-4)

God gives *according to* His fullness, glory and excellence. He lacks nothing so naturally His blessings are complete and whole. God wants to share His divine nature with all of us as we come to know and accept Him. However as His children, we tend to give *based upon* because we do not know the Father, our importance to Him, and our position in life. Sure I can loan this much or give this much, but I have to make sure that I have enough until next payday. I will be there, but I only have so much time to spare. There is not a whole lot I can do. I am not as smart. I lack resources. I am not capable of completing the task or I am afraid to start. Based upon who I am, what I have or what I can do, I can only do so much! This is the

Do We Resemble Our Father

result of a lack of vision and faith. We focus on ourselves and our situation rather than focusing on God who is all and has given all.

However, there are those who understand the gift of giving. There are those who understand they have an unlimited resource in God. These are children of God who do not give *based upon* but *according to* their Father in Heaven. They are concerned with the will of God more than their own needs. They do not focus on an idea that something is missing from their life, but God is made perfect in their weaknesses. True Christians know that God is love and hope for all ages. He is always with us and one day we will be with Him completely.

Remember the story of the Good Samaritan? He helped a man who was beaten on the side of the road. They were both from two different races and culture. But that did not matter. When the Samaritan saw the man, left alone to die, he felt compassion for him. First he tended to the man's wounds, and then gave him a lift to the next town. After purchasing a hotel room for the man to rest and get better, the Samaritan told the man in charge to get the man *anything* he needed, and whatever the bill came to, the

Do We Resemble Our Father

Samaritan would take care of when he returned. There are people today that go above and beyond the call of duty. Giving more than what is required. Not for profit or to seek attention, but working together to fill other people with hope. That by faith, they may also stand firm in their relationship with God.

"I have shown you in every way, by laboring like this, that you must support the weak. And remember the words of the Lord Jesus, that He said, 'It is more blessed to give than to receive.'" (Acts 20:35)

Just as God gives in completion, it says in John 1:16 that we *all* have received. Since the dawn of creation, no one is left out. Everyone has the opportunity to be included in reflecting God's glory. In 2 Corinthians 3:18, Paul states we all reflect the glory of the Lord with uncovered faces, and that same glory which comes from the Lord in Spirit, transforms us into His likeness in a greater degree of glory! God nature and true character is seen through His children. Not the speculation of selfishness that Satan wants to portray of God.

2 Corinthians 8:12-13 says, *"Whatever you give is acceptable if you give it eagerly. And give <u>according to</u>*

Do We Resemble Our Father

what you have, not what you do not have. Of course, I do not mean your giving should make life easy for others and hard for yourselves but there should be some equality." Paul instructs believers in Corinth to give from a cheerful heart. God will provide the resources and the amount needed to give to others. If little is given, our focus is on ourselves. Too much and the person receiving may become dependent on the giver rather than God. So what do we believe we have, as children of God, to give?

When we fail to understand and realize what God has given us according to His grace, as sinners we remain separate from Him. Our loving Father comes to us asking 'how', 'why' or 'who'. After Adam and Eve disobeyed God, God questioned Adam saying, "Who told you that you were naked?" God was asking Adam who told him that he was lacking anything for these reasons:

1) God wanted Adam to see that He supplied him with everything he needed to live.

2) God wanted to give Adam the opportunity to accept responsibility for his actions.

3) God wanted Adam to realize the relationship that was severed between him and God because of Adam's sin.

Do We Resemble Our Father

4) God wanted Adam to see what happened the moment he decided to do things his way, rather than depend on God.

Being responsible is accepting credit for the choice that was made whether it was right or wrong. As a result of Adam's sin, he damaged his relationship with God, and chose to blame Eve rather than accept responsibility for his own actions.

Remember what happened with Job when Satan took everything from his life? His wife told him to curse God, which he did not do, but Job complained about his situation. Before God blessed Job with what was taken from him, God pointed out Job's weaknesses and reminded Job who he is dealing with. God was pleased with Job overall because even though Job would spiritually stumble, he would not turn his back on God.

Now what is it that we are instructed to do? Who told us that we lack anything, or not capable of completing our part? More importantly, why do we look at what we think is missing more so than believing in what we have? Why does God have to prove Himself? What source has the audacity to challenge God and His children who ought *to*

Do We Resemble Our Father

know what their Father is about? How do we feel as parents when our children do not believe in us or we do not believe in them? Imagine if everyone gave up believing. What about excuses from children, or adults, that are given not to complete a task, and we know they are capable? Decisions are made that can be selfish, or focused on how it will impact the person. However, knowing we have the bible as a guide to living victoriously, what will be our response or choice? Do we allow Jesus to show us the way?

God has given us free will. According to 2 Timothy 1:7, God also has given us power, love, and a sound mind. We have the ability to do the right thing. But, God does not want a forced relationship with us, so it pleases Him when we **choose** a life with Him. Life choices are ours to make. When we choose a path apart from God, He becomes a concerned parent. God questions us, for our benefit, to deepen our understanding of:

- Who God is.
- What He has given us.
- What happens when we separate ourselves from Him?

Yes all of us will be challenged and faced with temptations. But Jesus understands what we experience. As

Do We Resemble Our Father

it was mentioned in Hebrews 2:18, Jesus overcame sin that we would not have to endure it alone. In the face of adversity, will you focus on who is telling you what God is not or does not have? Will your surroundings be the guide of what is directing your actions? Or according to the word of God, will you accept who you are and what you have in Christ and know that God has already won the battle?

Chapter 4

Fear versus Focus

The scripture 1 Thessalonians 5:9 says, that God through our Lord Jesus Christ, chose to save us, **not** to pour out His anger on us. In Isaiah 54:7-8, God reveals His response when we sin against Him- He turns His face from us. Yet, with great compassion and everlasting love, He takes us back! In verse 15, God continues to say, "If anyone comes to attack you, it is **not** because I have sent them." God does not attack us, but the sin within. The Creator does not destroy creation, but the **sin** that has destroyed His creation. God is the 'fountain of life' as stated in Psalms 36:9. The Creator *is* life in Himself and His life did not come from another. God gives life, creates the creature, and renews the face of the Earth. All life stems from Him and *remains* dependent on Him. Even so, mankind chooses to exist in an amazing dichotomy, or contrast, because we are God's most precious living thought of creativity, yet we want independence from Him.

Clearly, Jesus spoke of God as having life in Himself. (John 5:26) God is the One who gives life to all things (1

Do We Resemble Our Father

Timothy 6:13) No creature has life in itself. All life is a gift of God-eternal life through Jesus Christ. God and life are one; therefore, as He is the giver of life, we belong to Him. Not only does God want us to learn about Him through Jesus, but as we grow, God wants us to focus on living the life of Jesus. It is not the goal to live life defeated and depressed, but to be victorious with the joy of the Lord.

Throughout Jesus' ministry with the disciples, His main focus for them was relationship building. If they are going to spread the news of God's kingdom, getting to know Him and the Father was a priority. In Matthew 12:50, Jesus said that those who do the will of my Father *are* his brothers, sisters and mothers. This must be in the hearts of all. This is the kingdom of God. Nothing else matters.

In Matthew 14, Jesus knew when Peter walked out on the water to Him; Peter would not fail as long as he focused on Christ. The moment Peter gave more attention to his surroundings than on Christ; he gave doubt and fear an opportunity to enter his thoughts which would lead to sin. He became unsure that he could continue his journey and God would be unable to help. If Peter just remained focused, he would see that Jesus did not give in to His

Do We Resemble Our Father

surroundings. Jesus remained victorious and the same would have happened for Peter. As Jesus called Peter to come to Him, Peter had everything he needed to complete the task. With each step, God was *already* making provisions for him. Peter was accomplishing his task. But Peter began to look and think about the situation around him... *What if I do not make it? Will Jesus be able to save me from the storm?* When we are assigned a job, there may be 'bumps in the road'. The spiritual ability to walk "two feet" on the water should have affirmed to Peter that he was with Christ where there is no failure! However, before we criticize Peter, note the sincerity and depth of Peter's faith with this proclamation: HE GOT OUT OF THE BOAT! Likewise, do we have the faith, **"To get out of the boat(s) of complacency?"** How often do we "second guess" our decisions to end destructive life patterns?

How will I make it?... These problems are too much for me or anyone else to handle.

We allow the situation to overwhelm and defeat us. What barriers are attempting to keep us from finishing our goals? Are we giving more focus to what we feel we do not have, or what we think is lacking? In the midst of trouble,

Do We Resemble Our Father

do we hold on to God's unchanging hand? Do we build our hopes on things eternal or 'sinking sand' ideas? It is more than believing. It is accepting who we are. Do you know who you are and what you have?

When God is left out of the situation, we fail to utilize our most complete resource. As Peter began to sink, he cried out and Jesus immediately saved him. Jesus then asked Peter why he doubted Him with so little faith. Another situation arises. Jesus told Peter and no one else to come out to Him. What if one of the other disciples wanted to come out of the boat. Would they have waited for Jesus' command, or started on their own before Peter began to sink? When we make mistakes, God is there at a moment's notice to rescue us, because He loves us dearly. All thanks and praise be to God that we can call on Him when we fall! But we need to call on our Father in all situations. The good times and the bad. If God has given us what we need to survive, why do we second guess what He has provided? Throughout bible history as God instructed His people for different tasks, similar responses emerged:

- Why me Lord? I lack the resources.
- I am not ready.

Do We Resemble Our Father

- I doubt that I can do this.
- The task is too much.
- The burden is too great.

The above *self-doubt* emotions *underscore and fuel* non-productive *thought* processes which weaken our faith; as a result, we give in to situations, environment, and people, anything that supports our actions controlled by fear or doubt. Maybe we think we cannot operate in the same manner as Jesus. In Matthew 11:27 Jesus says, that God has entrusted Him with *everything*! No one knows *Jesus as well* as the Father and no one knows the Father as well as Jesus *and to whom* Jesus chooses *to reveal* the Father. Jesus has all power, yet His authority was challenged by the church with their questions of doubt. To operate in the image and likeness of the Father is to **know** Him by what Christ has revealed, and the Holy Spirit has affirmed.

Each of us has a designed purpose in life, blessings to give and receive, and miracles to perform. But maybe we are not aware of our gift or not satisfied with what it is. We believe it is not flashy enough. Summarily, when our focus shifts from God's will to personal appeal, the desire

Do We Resemble Our Father

"shifts" to please the people rather than teach the people. This practice encourages *growth in numbers* rather than *growing in Grace*! Whether we desire a large or small ministry, our "walking on water" trial could be forgiving someone closest to you that has betrayed you. Yes, we must be spiritually clear on the call. Doubting or being unsure can expand into fear! Consequently, fear or doubt of doing what God instructs us to do; we attempt to complete something different hoping that the outcome will be positive as well. Doing a different job may seem less difficult, but your gifts and talents are not being used. We tend to lose "sight" of the call and sense of purpose. This may lead to participating in **much**, but completing **little**. For example, not everyone is called to preach. This is also the same for other professions as well. Not everyone is called to be a lawyer, physician, athlete, or work in politics. Unfortunately there are people who work in these professions for money, social status, basically all the wrong reasons. Since this is not a natural ability or talent, it is possible their position, or the work they produce, may cause hurt, harm, danger, or difficulty to themselves or the people around them. Some may have lived a full life

Do We Resemble Our Father

without seeing any harm done at all. It is possible they missed their opportunity to operate in God's image and likeness. We should not sacrifice our spiritual inheritance for physical desires. Especially since God is able to fill us with the desires of our heart. (Psalms 37:4) With the story of Moses, God spoke about His relationship with Moses' ancestors to show Moses the importance of his spiritual heritage with God. Also God had to reassure Moses that even with his speech impediment, He would help Moses and tell him exactly what to say. Moses gave into fear and used his inabilities to "excuse" his actions. Therefore, he felt that he could not speak to the people or Pharaoh *because of* his stuttering. Moses kept putting obstacles in front of himself, before finally allowing God to lead him to victory. The bible has record account of many men and women with God-given purposes. Whether or not they gave into doubt, one thing was certain; God always provided. Let us be mindful that God will give us everything we need to complete our purpose/task, even when it seems humanly impossible. We complain about our situation, but what happens when God comes to rescue us? Fear or focus will determine our direction in how we live. God has provided a

Do We Resemble Our Father

way out by Jesus sacrificing His life on the cross. We are freed from what has kept us under control. We do not like this because now we are responsible for our own actions. No longer can we use something else as an excuse for our mistakes or misunderstanding. When the children of Israel were freed from Pharaoh's captivity, they complained about their situation on their way to the Promised Land and how their lives were better off in Egypt. Yes, there are those who would rather live under the control of a negative situation than be guided by God. So that the responsibility of their actions would rely on someone else. Furthermore, as Satan told Eve that she and Adam would be like gods knowing good and evil, naturally, we want to know the future so that we can plan ahead or be prepared. Not everyone is accustomed to surprises. We may have to step out of that comfort zone. If you are caught in a mundane condition, are you willing to step out on faith and allow Jesus to finish what He has started with you? Start by knowing and accepting who you are, remember what is in store for you in eternity, and pray to remain focused on God. Do not allow Satan to rob you of your heritage!

More and more as our society focuses for an easier

Do We Resemble Our Father

lifestyle, we lose people with God given abilities to improve our way of life living together, because less effort is required to give from ourselves. This is not to say that working hard is the only way. We must be careful not to focus or be dependent on an easy life, but find out how we can complete our part by being available in God's plan where others are not able. God wants to reveal Himself to the world through the rich and the poor alike. *Spiritually, when you accept who you are and where you come from, that state of existence will project in everything you do.* There are many cultures all over the world. Many of which have different accents in their speech and dialect. It is who they are because of where they are from. What we see is the beauty of difference in God's creation. Variety is the spice of life. In all things of this world that is contrasted, what about that which binds all of mankind together? Jesus came to reveal the Father to the world and show us how to *resemble* God in our lives. That which is in Jesus *is* within us as well! The time approaches, that only the Father knows, when He will come for those who resemble the "Fruit of His Spirit."

Do We Resemble Our Father

Chapter 5

Father's Day

There are many special days that occur throughout the year. One in particular is father's day-the day when men who represent a father figure are honored in celebration. They range from uncles, stepfathers, male cousins, grandfathers, and even males that volunteer in big brother programs. The role of a father is important in the family unit. Their spiritual role is likened to God, our Father in Heaven. Just as God created us in His image and likeness, He wants man to be a representation of a true father on Earth as it is in Heaven. In Genesis 1:28, God gave man dominion over the Earth. Being a father shows leadership and one who guides. Also a father is one who creates, or is the foundation of a family line. He shows responsibility, discipline with love, integrity, forgiveness, encouragement, trust, honor, strength, and protection. Most importantly, a father raises his children in truth and fairness, not anger.

Throughout the bible, God shows these qualities within

Do We Resemble Our Father

Himself as the true Father. As males, we have the ability to **resemble** and actively portray the same qualities because we are created in God's image and likeness. God shows forgiveness in Isaiah 43: 25. God says, *"I-yes, I alone-will blot out your sins for my own sake and will never think of them again."*

God demonstrates strength and protection in verse 13 of the same chapter... *"From eternity to eternity I am God. No one can snatch anyone out of my hand. No one can undo what I have done."*

In Isaiah 44:24 God states as a Creator, *"This is what the Lord says-your Redeemer and Creator: I am the Lord, who made all things. I alone stretched out the heavens. Who was with me when I made the earth?"*

God is family oriented. In Isaiah 45:10 the Lord says, *"How terrible it would be if a newborn baby said to its father, 'Why was I born?' Or if it said to its mother, 'Why did you make me this way?'"*

God gives generously to His children. In Isaiah 45:11 God says, *"This is what the Lord says - the Holy One of Israel and your Creator: 'Do you question what I do for my children? Do you give me orders about the work of my*

Do We Resemble Our Father

hands? I am the One who made the earth and created people to live in it.'"

Our Father is trustworthy and responsible. In Isaiah 46:3-5 God says, *"Listen to me, descendants of Jacob, all of you who remain in Israel. I have cared for you since you were born. Yes, I carried you <u>before</u> you were born. I will be your God throughout your lifetime-until your hair is white with age. I made you, and I will care for you. I will carry you along and save you."*

God gives encouragement to His children. In Isaiah 41:10 God says, *"Do not be afraid, for I am with you. Do not be discouraged, for I am your God. I will strengthen you and help you. I will hold you up with my victorious right hand."*

God is dedicated to providing all we need as His children. He is fair and just. Isaiah 60:19-22 God says, *"No longer will you need the sun to shine by day, nor the moon to give its light by night, for the Lord your God will be your everlasting light, and your God will be your glory. Your sun will never set; your moon will never go down. For the Lord will be your everlasting light. Your days of mourning will come to an end. All your people will be righteous. They*

Do We Resemble Our Father

will possess their land forever, for I will plant them there with my own hands in order to bring myself glory. The smallest family will become a thousand people, and the tiniest group will become a mighty nation. At the right time, I, the Lord, will make it happen."

God proudly accepts us as His own with important recognition. Isaiah 66:22 God says, *"As surely as my new heavens and earth will remain, so will you always be my people, with a name that will <u>never</u> disappear."*

In Proverbs 3:12, the Lord disciplines those whom He loves as a father should raise his children according to Ephesians 6:4. Because of who God is, He is highly honored above all. Revelations 1:8 God says, *"I am the Alpha and Omega-the beginning and the end. I am the One who is, who always was, and who is still to come- the Almighty One."*

As God is the true Father, we have been told and shown of His love. (John 3:16) How can we display our love for Him as His children in preparation for His day? What does His day mean to Him?

The Son of the Father, our Lord and Savior Jesus Christ taught us exactly what love is all about. In Matthew 22:37-

Do We Resemble Our Father

39 Jesus says, *"You must love the Lord your God with all your heart, all your soul, and all your mind. This is the first and greatest commandment. A second and equally important: Love your neighbor as yourself."* Jesus taught us in Matthew 6:24 that God must be our first love and not money. We cannot be equally devoted to both. We will love one being devoted to it while hating and despise the other. What occupies your thoughts or efforts, God or money? Basically, are you dependent on God to supply your needs, or that next paycheck to pay bills, and support your lifestyle? Mark 10:25 says, *it is easier for a camel to go through the eye of a needle, then for a rich person to enter the Kingdom of God.*

We show our love to the Father by accepting and obeying His commandments through Jesus. In return, both the Father and Jesus will love us and reveal God's kingdom to the world through us. (John14:21) If we do not accept Jesus into our lives as in John 5:41-44, we do not have the love of the Father within us. Remember that Jesus is the way, the truth and the life. He is the only path to the Father because Jesus and the Father operate in the same frame of mind. A husband and wife express God's love in marriage

Do We Resemble Our Father

when they become one in spirit and operate in togetherness and not division. They compliment and teach one another with positive influences. The couple continues to grow in Christ daily to solidify their bond. The wife submits to her husband, and the husband gives his life to her as Christ gave His life to the church. (Ephesians 5:22-25) Correction is done out of love, wisdom, and respect. They are a foundation and representation of the Trinity led by God's Holy Spirit.

John 13:35 says, that showing our love to one another will prove to the world that we are Jesus' disciples. This is tough considering the times we are living in. People are concerned with their own wants and needs. We worry about paying bills, the next paycheck, working enough hours, making it *to* work, making it to *tomorrow*, healthcare, education system, schools, religion, civil rights, civil wars on terrorism, budget cuts, upper-middle-lower management stress, investments, stocks, friends, family, enemies, strangers, our way of life or life in general, eating, drinking, entertainment, neighbors, communities, the weather, global economy, our beliefs, morals and values, or retirement. The list is endless; however there may be those who live

Do We Resemble Our Father

without caring. Either way sometimes presents a tough job in expressing God's love. Ephesians 5:1-2 says, *"Imitate God in everything you do, because you are His dear children. Live a life filled with love, following the example of Christ. He loved us and offered himself as a sacrifice for us, a pleasing aroma to God."*

Jesus wants our love to be genuine. In John 21:15-17, Jesus asks Peter three times if he loved Him and if so, spread the gospel. Do we love our Father? Do we really love Him? Are we His children? Then let us show the world our Father within us. Let us tell the world about His true nature. Satan has told lies about our Father and His kingdom to keep us separated from Him.

So what does Father's day mean to God? Before I discuss this, being a father has been the most rewarding and challenging experience for me. I have found myself always wanting to provide for my children. From a young age about nine, I knew I would have children someday. Also, I loved helping out with babies. Even today the sound of children's voices are music to my ears. I look forward to father's day out of curiosity and eagerness. Not looking for the most or least expensive gift, but how my children

Do We Resemble Our Father

express their love for me.

This is a day that Jesus is preparing for as well. In John 14:1-3 Jesus tells his disciples, *"Do not let your hearts be troubled. Trust in God, and trust in me. There is more than enough room in my Father's home. If this were not so, would I have told you that I am going to prepare a place for you? When everything is ready, I will come and get you, so that you will always be with me where I am."*

With great anticipation, our Father patiently waits for the day that we will be reunited with Him. Just like in the story of the prodigal son when the father welcomed his son with great happiness. The time will come when God will send His Son, Jesus to bring us home. Remember, Jesus is the way. God in advance adopted us into His own family by bringing us to Himself through Jesus Christ. (Ephesians 1:5) It was the *only* way to repair the damage done to the family of God. Also, God has shown love beyond description. He is coming for those who have been expressing their love for Him, His children who accept Him as the Father, a desire to be known and associated with His family, and those who allowed God to reveal Himself through their lives. This will be the greatest family reunion,

Do We Resemble Our Father

ever. There will be a huge celebration as a new Heaven and Earth will be created by God for us to live with Him forever. As another expression of love, God will wipe every tear from our eyes, and there will be no more death, sorrow, crying, or pain. All these things are gone forever. (Revelation 21:1-4) That which sought to destroy us will be thrown into the lake of fire, **never again to come between the Father and His children**. (Revelation 20:10)

Are we displaying God's image? When the world views us, as Christians, are our morals and values the same likeness of God? Jesus has shown us how to walk in God's ordered steps. God's Holy Spirit will teach, lead, guide, all things that God gives to accomplish His will. It comes down to us and the choice we decide to make. Do we resemble our Father? What we portray to the world will tell God the answer whether or not we want to be with Him. I love my Father, how about you?

ABOUT THE AUTHOR

Rodney K. Adams was born and raised in Chicago, Illinois. He has served in the U.S. Air Force, Illinois National Guard, and the U.S. Army. Although the military has been a way of life for Rodney, he received his license and is training in ministry. Presently, the Adams family resides near Savannah, Georgia.

www.ingramcontent.com/pod-product-compliance
Lightning Source LLC
Chambersburg PA
CBHW032018290426
44109CB00013B/701